# This GODLY Coloring & Activity

# Workbook Belongs To:

_____

# GOD IS LOVE
## Coloring and Activity Workbook

Written by: Carline Constant and Gregory Constant
Illustrated by: Leena Shariq

Subtitle: Christian Coloring & Activity Workbook Inspirational Faith Based-
We Pray, Pray, Pray with Hanna, Grandma, & Caleb Series

Text Copyright © 2025 by Carline Constant and Gregory Constant
Illustrations Copyright © 2025 by Leena Shariq
A Sprinkle Joy Publishing Book

For information contact us online at: www.sprinklejoybooks.com

Summary:

***GOD IS LOVE Coloring and Activity Workbook*** is FUN for kids, families and people of all ages to flourish in faith. A companion to the series of books in We Pray, Pray, Pray with Hanna, Grandma, & Caleb, together, these GODLY books and workbook show engaging inspirational scenes with activities to motivate and develop Bible Habits to grow trusting in God. Let the Spirit of God direct our lives in understanding Christian values, practicing virtues for faithful living.

Subjects:
CYAC: 1. Faith Based Inspirational Christian Coloring & Activity Workbook-Realistic Fiction. 2. Kids Godly Morals & Values Virtues Prayer Workbook. 3. Family Grandchild Grandparent-Picture Workbook & Book Series-Realistic Fiction. 4. Kids Spiritual Life Lessons-Christianity. 5. Christian Bible Habits. 6. Pray With Hanna Grandma & Caleb Christian Series. 7. African American Christian Family-Realistic Fiction Book & Workbook.

Identifiers:
Paperback Workbook ISBN # 979-8-9921558-2-2
Hardcover ISBN # 979-8-9921558-3-9

Library of Congress Control Number: 2024925918

Companion Books:
*Hanna's Blessings, I am Thankful, Pray at Mealtime, Forgive Others.*

All scripture quotations marked (GNT) are from the Good News Bible Translation in Today's English Version-Copyright © 1993 by American Bible Society. Used by permission.

Printed in the United States of America
LCCN Imprint: Sprinkle Joy Publishing, New York.

10 9 8 7 6 5 4 3 2 1
First Edition: February 2025

Semi Realistic Art Style
For Ages 5-12

## Sprinkle Joy Publishing Books

**www.sprinklejoybooks.com**

# WITH GRATEFUL HEARTS TO GOD!

This workbook is dedicated to all children and families worldwide.

Thanks to Ms. Dolores Mary Fleck for editing this workbook.

Thanks to our family and friends for words of encouragement.

Thanks to God for the many blessings.

## TO GOD BE THE GLORY!

-Gregory Constant

- Carline Constant

 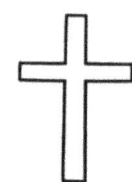  

# THERE IS ONE GOD, WHO IS FATHER, SON AND HOLY SPIRIT.

"Love is patient and kind."
(1 Corinthians 13:4 GNT)

"Love never gives up; and its faith, hope, and patience never fail. Love is eternal."
(1 Corinthians 13:7-8 GNT)

 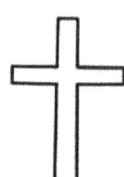  

"Out of the fullness of His grace He has blessed us all, giving us one blessing after another."
(John 1:16 GNT)

# www.sprinklejoybooks.com

# GOD IS LOVE
## Coloring and Activity Workbook

Written by
**Carline Constant and Gregory Constant**

Sprinkle Joy
Publishing

Grandma prays softly in church, "God, thank You for loving me and my family. We have faith in You, God! Please help us to always turn our faces and hearts to You, God, in the name of Your Son, Jesus Christ."

Directions: Read the Bible verse, answer the question and color the cross.

➜**What does the following Bible verse mean?**

# "We love because God first loved us."
## ( 1 John 4:19 GNT)

**The Bible verse means** _____

_____

_____

_____

"Hanna, we are grateful for God's many blessings in our lives, like good health, family, a joyful heart, food, clothing, a warm home, friends and much more," Grandma says.

I kneel and pray,
"God, I'm grateful for Your blessings,
a loving family, my new friends
and a warm home.
I thank You, God, for loving me and
helping me to be a blessing."

PRAISE GOD!
"How good it is to give thanks to You, O LORD, to sing in Your honor, O Most High God, to proclaim Your constant love every morning and Your faithfulness every night, with the music of stringed instruments and with melody on the harp. Your mighty deeds, O LORD, make me glad; because of what You have done, I sing for joy!"
(Psalm 92: 1-4 GNT)

→ **How do you praise God?**

# ♡ GOD IS LOVE ♡

FATHER     compassionate     grace

SON     righteous     mercy

HOLYSPIRIT     divine     faithful

King     gracious     kind

Jesus     joy     hope

Almighty     love

Lord     peace

creator     provider

trinity     **OUR**     sacred

eternity     **LOVING**     blessed

holy     **GOD**     good

truth     powerful

righteous     unity

savior     loving     infinity     merciful

great     rock     spirit     protector

shepherd     refuge     wisdom     shield

merciful     Eternal

goodness     maker     patience

blessings     healer     forgiveness

unconditional     helper     loving

worthy     gift     dependable

renewal     giver     forgiver

➡ **My words for GOD:** _____ _____ _____

# ♡ LOVE GOD ♡

Directions: Find and circle the following hidden words.

| | | |
|---|---|---|
| CHRISTIANS | FAITH | GOD |
| GRACE | HOPE | JOY |
| ~~LOVE~~ | PRAYER | |

| | | | | | | | | | | | |
|---|---|---|---|---|---|---|---|---|---|---|---|
| M | B | P | W | Z | V | B | S | D | R | J | R |
| P | Y | E | G | B | M | R | O | V | I | Y | K |
| Y | I | D | T | R | Z | G | V | D | Q | K | E |
| P | S | A | S | E | D | X | A | E | U | Z | C |
| S | N | A | I | T | S | I | R | H | C | C | A |
| Z | J | X | L | Z | W | B | K | H | O | X | R |
| U | M | X | P | D | L | U | S | B | J | P | G |
| L | J | W | J | R | C | O | Z | R | F | L | E |
| Y | H | Q | V | U | A | N | V | D | W | G | I |
| A | O | Z | Z | L | Z | Y | L | E | A | U | H |
| W | Y | J | H | B | S | Y | E | T | K | A | Q |
| A | W | M | F | A | I | T | H | R | E | A | L |

**"My heart praises the Lord; my soul is glad because of God my Savior."**
**(Luke 1:46-47 GNT)**

Sprinkle Joy
Publishing
www.sprinklejoybooks.com

## GOD IS LOVE CROSSWORD PUZZLE

**Directions:** Complete the crossword puzzle below.
Use the following words across or down.

| Christians | God | Hope | Love |
|---|---|---|---|
| Faith | Grace | Joy | Pray |

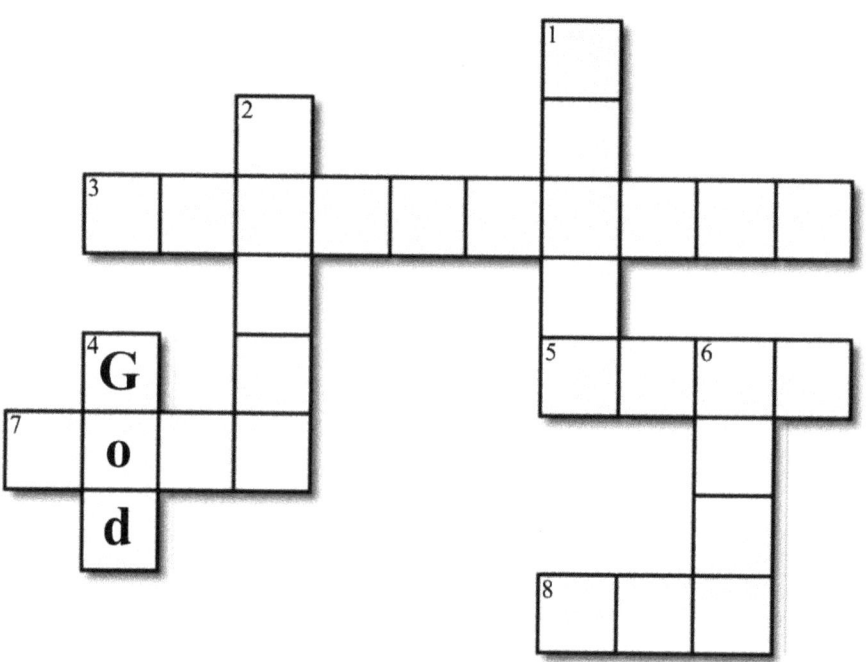

**Across**

**3.** People who believe in Jesus Christ our Savior, the Son of God. _____.

**5.** To trust and have confidence in God. _____.

**7.** Putting others before yourself, seeing good qualities in people and valuing them. _____.

**8.** A feeling of happiness, a fruit of the Spirit. _____.

**Down**

**1.** To believe and trust in the hope and blessings of God. _____.

**2.** Free gift, and favor from God working in you. _____.

**4.** Almighty creator of the world and everything in it. ____**God**____.

**6.** To speak sharing your thoughts and listen to God. _____.

Sprinkle Joy
Publishing
www.sprinklejoybooks.com

# GOD IS LOVE : BELIEVE IN GOD

Directions: Find and circle the following hidden words.

| | | |
|---|---|---|
| BELIEVE | ~~PATIENCE~~ | VALUES |
| GRATEFUL | PEACE | VIRTUES |
| MERCY | PRAYER | |

| | | | | | | | | | | | |
|---|---|---|---|---|---|---|---|---|---|---|---|
| T | G | R | A | T | E | F | U | L | K | O | L |
| B | C | P | V | N | Z | V | E | C | A | E | P |
| Q | B | V | J | Y | M | O | E | B | P | W | S |
| V | I | R | T | U | E | S | C | I | X | R | N |
| Q | N | S | D | J | H | A | L | V | L | L | P |
| R | V | X | G | U | G | B | A | H | D | E | L |
| Y | Y | C | R | E | M | L | S | A | A | E | B |
| T | X | D | S | P | U | F | W | K | J | T | O |
| P | A | O | W | E | M | O | R | O | F | H | E |
| P | D | E | S | X | K | Q | V | G | D | K | I |
| R | E | Y | A | R | P | H | C | I | G | B | R |
| F | P | A | T | I | E | N | C | E | I | D | O |

Sprinkle Joy
Publishing
www.sprinklejoybooks.com

## GOD IS LOVE CROSSWORD PUZZLE

**Directions:** Complete the crossword puzzle below.
Use the following words across or down.

| believe | mercy | peace | values |
| greatful | patience | prayer | virtues |

**Across**

**2.** To be thankful and appreciate good things in life. _____

**4.** To trust, have faith that something exists that is true and good. _____

**6.** Good characteristics we demonstrate, actions or behaviors to benefit someone else. _____

**8.** Qualities that motivate our character and behavior that help us make decisions. _____

**Down**

**1.** To be kind and gentle and not give up hope. _____

**3.** To forgive and not punish someone. _____ (mercy)

**5.** To talk to God and listen to God. _____

**7.** To live in harmony with no violence or war. _____

# ROUTINE ADDITION AND SUBTRACTION MATH BIBLE CHALLENGE

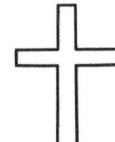

**Directions:** Solve the following and show your work.

7 - 3 = ____

25 + 3 = ____

82 + 6 = ____

5 + 9 ____ 18 - 3
(Circle one =, >,<)

42 + ____ = 64

562 - ____ = 82

52 + 9 = ____

255 + 17 = ____

```
  36            297            57            592
+              +              -              -
   2             13            46             34
____          ____          ____          ____

____          ____          ____          ____
```

In the box below complete the **addition number line** and write the answer. 3+4=☐

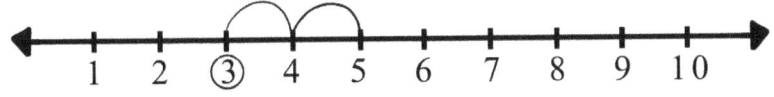

# FUN BIBLE FRACTIONS!

**Directions:** Read the fraction and circle the correct answer for the equivalent fraction.
Next, draw the fraction on the line next to each.
Example: ½=2/4 ▨☐1/2 ▨▨☐☐2/4

**1/2**

3/4 _____

OR

3/6 _____


**1/3**

1/8 _____

OR

4/12 _____


**2/6**

3/9 _____

OR

4/12 _____


Add the fractions and write the answer.

$\frac{1}{6} + \frac{4}{6} =$ ☐

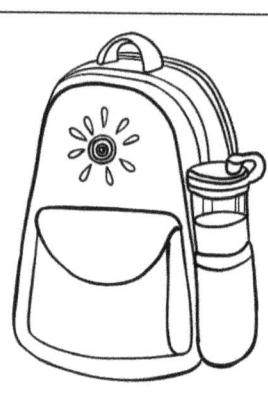

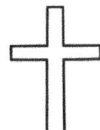

# MULTIPLICATION & DIVISION MATH BIBLE ROUTINE

**Directions:** Solve the following and show your work.

$8 \times \underline{\quad} = 64$

$82 \times 3 = \underline{\quad}$

$52 \times 5 = \underline{\quad}$

$25 \div 5 = \underline{\quad}$

$36 \div 7 = \underline{\quad}$

$98 \times 4 = \underline{\quad}$

$7\overline{)21}$

$3\overline{)28}$

$9\overline{)2710}$

$$\begin{array}{r} 13 \\ \times \quad 3 \\ \hline \end{array}$$

$$\begin{array}{r} 245 \\ \times \quad 2 \\ \hline \end{array}$$

$$\begin{array}{r} 523 \\ \times \quad 27 \\ \hline \end{array}$$

In the box below, **draw an <u>array</u>** for 4 x 6 and write the answer. 4x6 = ⬚

# ROUTINE MATH WORD PROBLEMS

**Directions:** Read and solve each word problem below to find the answer. On the blank line, create your own word problem and solve it. Remember to show your work.

1. 152 Bibles were ordered for our church Bible study group. When members from another church decided to join our Bible study group, an additional order of 22 was placed. What is the total amount of Bibles ordered?

2. A box has 24 Bibles in it. The youth group leader gives 15 away to teenagers. How many Bibles are left in the box?

3. It's Christmas Eve, the church choir has 42 vocal members. Two dozen active members gathered to go caroling around the community this special night. How many members are left at the church.

4. For 9 days, Grandma prayed at least 3 times daily, morning, noon and night. How many times did Grandma pray?

5. Write your own word problem below and solve it.

_____

_____

Sprinkle Joy
Publishing
www.sprinklejoybooks.com

# OUR MORNING PRAYER ☼

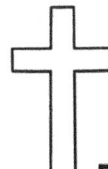

Directions: fill in the blanks using the words in the box.

| bless | please | day |
|-------|--------|-----|
| night | love | always |

God, You _____ me so much.

You're with me _____ and _____ .

I want to love You _____ ,

In all I do and say,

I'll try to _____ You, God,

_____ me through this day.

I love You God. Amen.

**"Be joyful always, pray at all times, be thankful in all circumstances." (1 Thessalonians 5:16-18 GNT)**

Sprinkle Joy
Publishing
www.sprinklejoybooks.com

# GOD LOOKS AT YOUR HEART

Directions: Choose actions words from the box and add two of your own. Write actions that please God in the heart. Write actions that don't please God outside the heart.

→ Action Words:

| LOVE | FORGIVE | GREED | FIGHTS | _____ |
|------|---------|-------|--------|---------|
| LIES | FAITH | KINDNESS | REVENGE | _____ |

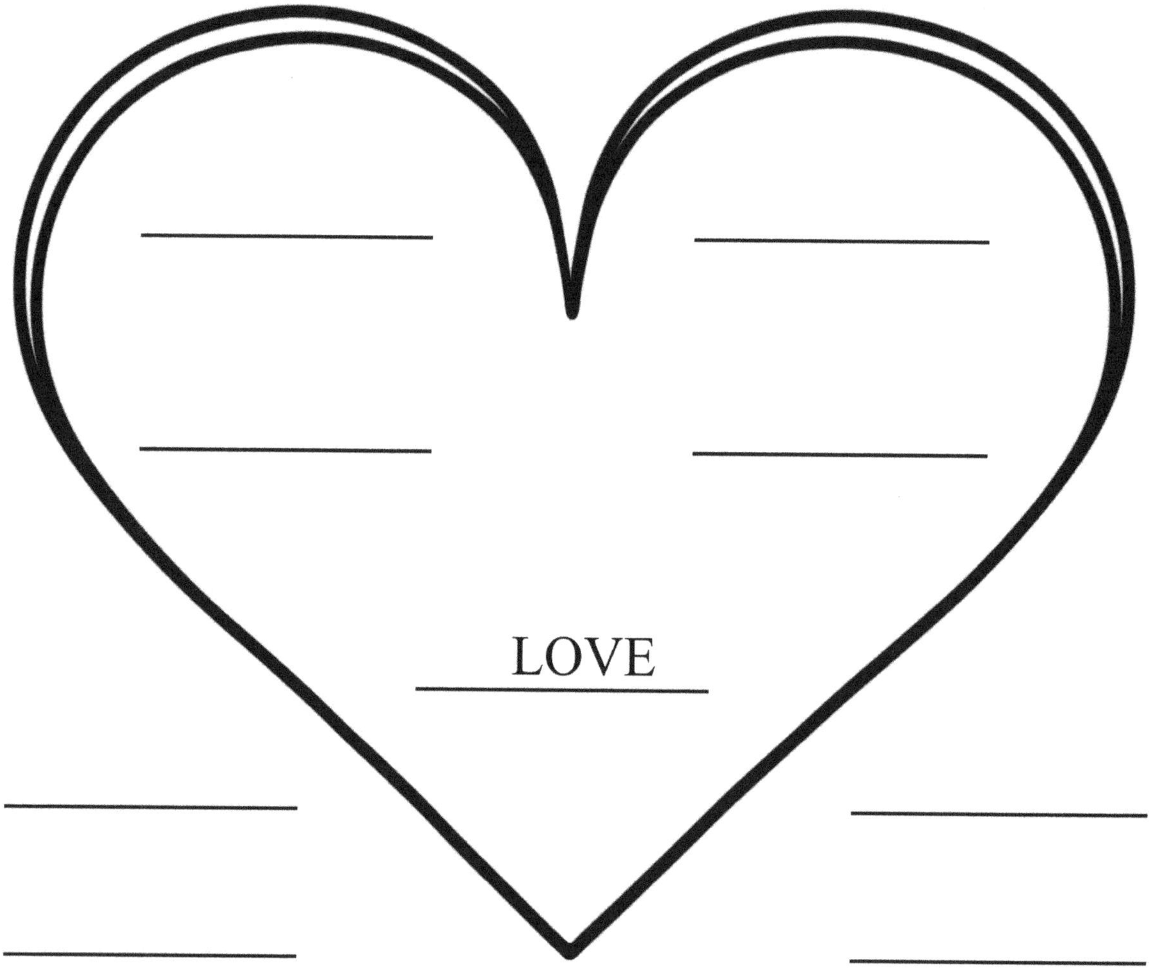

_____     _____

_____     _____

LOVE

_____          _____

_____          _____

FIGHTS

# GRACE BEFORE MEALS PRAYER
## WE ARE THANKFUL!

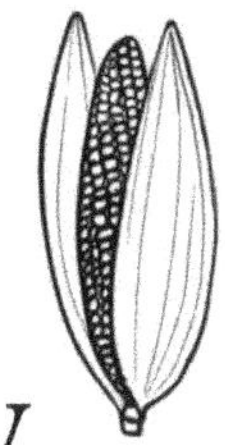

### Grace

Bless us, O Lord,
and these Thy gifts,
which we are about to
receive from Thy bounty,
through Christ our Lord.
Amen.

## Why is it good to pray before meals?

_____

_____

_____

_____

Name: _____

Directions: Complete the BE THANKFUL: PRAY TO GOD organizer writing words to describe why we have to be thankful and pray. Next, use the words to explain the reasons why we have to be thankful and pray on the lines below.

Details:
FAMILY

Details:

BE THANKFUL: PRAY TO GOD

Details:

Details:

Be thankful and pray because…

_____

_____

_____

"Give thanks to the LORD, for He is good."
(Psalm 107:1 GNT)

> *"For God loves the one, who gives gladly."*
> *(2 Corinthians 7-8 GNT)*

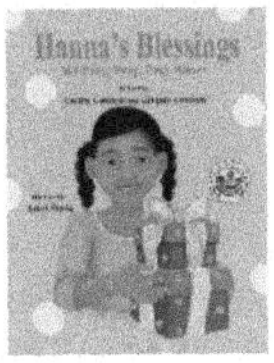

Cathy looks at me and says,
"But, I don't have a gift to give you, Hanna."
"That's okay," I tell her.
"Christmas is about sharing God's blessings.
These are my gifts to you and making a new friend is
your gift to me. Merry Christmas, Cathy!"

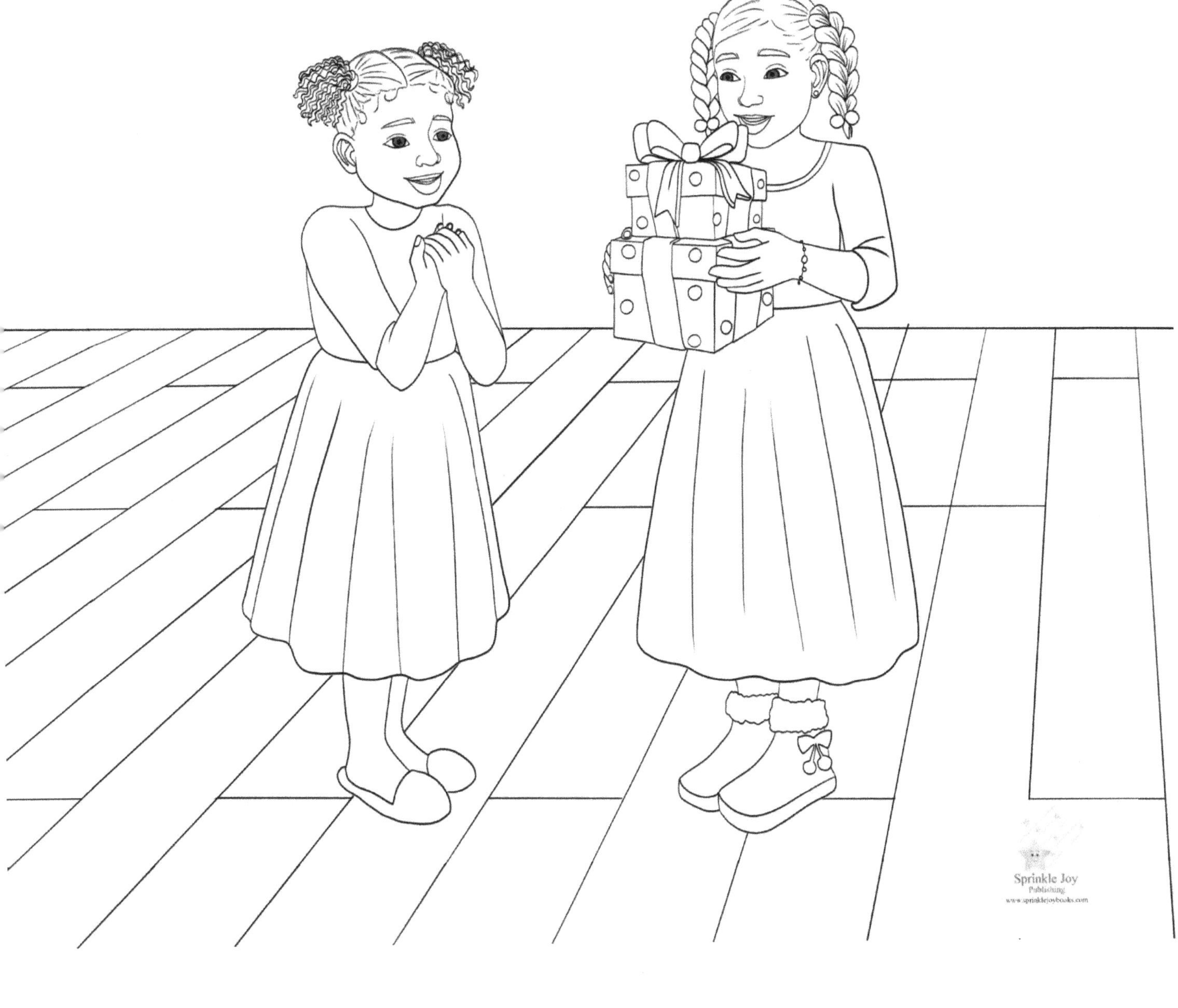

# "FOR GOD LOVED THE WORLD SO MUCH THAT HE GAVE HIS ONLY SON."
## (John 3:16 GNT)

► **How does God show you that He loves you?**

_____

_____

_____

► **What do the words: FAITH, HOPE, LOVE mean?**

_____

_____

_____

# Happy Birthday Jesus!

ON YOUR BIRTHDAY I WILL GIVE YOU:

_____

_____

_____

_____

_____

_____

_____

_____

_____

_____

_____

# MERRY CHRISTMAS

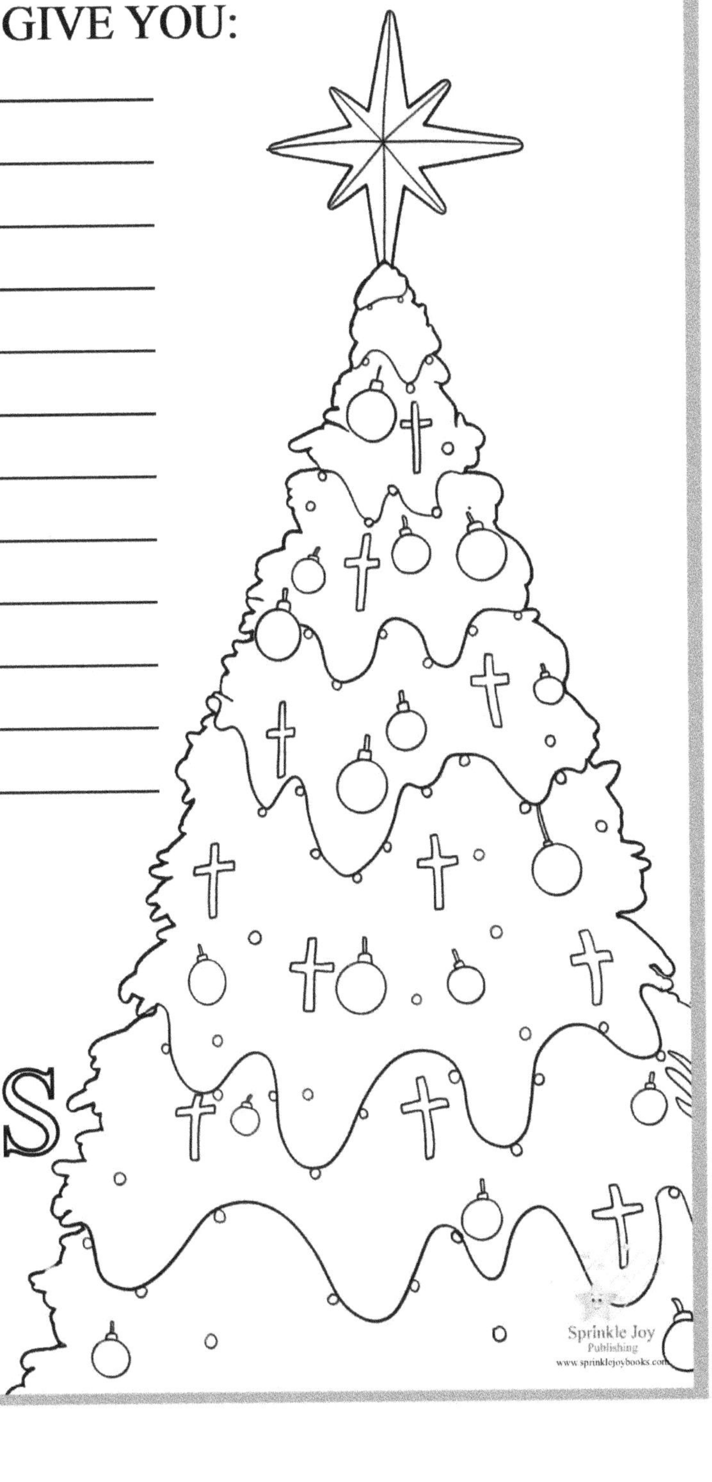

# Christ has Risen

⇨ **What does EASTER mean?**

Easter means: _____

_____

# PHONICS - PRONOUNCING THE WORD PRAY

Phonics – To recognize sounds and blend them together to form words.

→ Focus – The long vowel **a**/**a**/.

*Rule: When the letters **'ay'** are at the end of a word, the sound is /**ay**/.

The long vowel **a**/**a**/ with **'ay'** sound that the two letters next to each other make.
Pronounce, say **'ay'** in the word pray. Repeat, pray, pray, pray

<u>Directions:</u> Complete the words below, after, <u>read</u> the words out loud.
Then, <u>write</u> a sentence with a word that has the **'ay'** sound.
*Example: p<u>r</u>**ay**

1. _**ay**

2. _**ay**

3. __ __**ay**

4. __ __ay

5. __ __ __ay

6. __ __ __ay

Write sentence(s) with 2 words that have the **'ay'** sound.

_____

_____

# FUN WITH RHYMING WORDS

Rhyming words – are words that have similar ending sounds.

## Example: 'hat' and 'Pat'

Directions: Match the **rhyming** words. Then, write your own pairs
of words that rhyme.

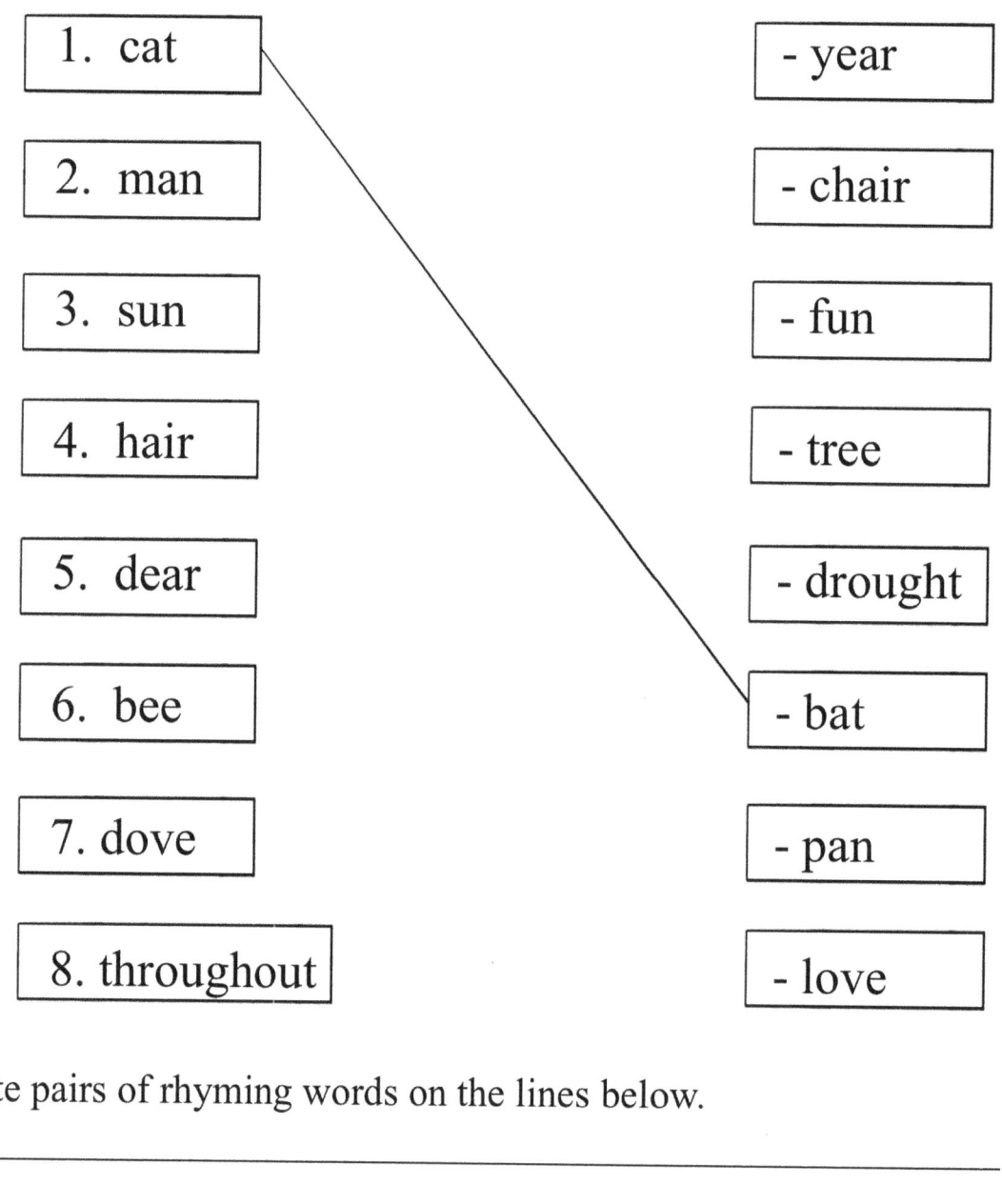

| | |
|---|---|
| 1. cat | - year |
| 2. man | - chair |
| 3. sun | - fun |
| 4. hair | - tree |
| 5. dear | - drought |
| 6. bee | - bat |
| 7. dove | - pan |
| 8. throughout | - love |

Write pairs of rhyming words on the lines below.

_____

_____

**"OUR FATHER IN HEAVEN:**
May Your Holy Name be honored; may Your Kingdom come; may Your will be done on earth as it is in heaven. Give us today the food we need. Forgive us the wrongs we have done, as we forgive the wrongs that others have done to us. Do not bring us to hard testing but keep us safe from the Evil One."
*(Matthew 6:9-13 GNT)*
*(Luke 11:2-4 GNT)*

After our prayers, Grandma took us to the park.
Omar and I loved to play freeze tag.
We ran, chased, tagged, froze, and unfroze.
It was so much fun.
"Caleb, you're my best pal!" Omar yelled.
"Way to go, Omar!" I cheered after he tagged me.

That night, I thought, *Omar is my best friend. I don't think he was being mean when he didn't choose me. He did say he wanted to give the other kids a chance to play. I can forgive Omar.*

**"Forgive others, and God will forgive you."**
**(Luke 6:37 GNT)**

# READING COMPREHENSION

**"Forgive others, and God will forgive you."**
(Luke 6:37 GNT)

Directions: Read the story and answer the following questions.

After school, I didn't speak to Omar. I couldn't stop thinking, *Omar is my best friend. But in gym, our only class together, when he was student leader, he didn't choose me to play freeze tag knowing how much I like the game.*
"Caleb, my buddy, we always play freeze tag when we're at the park with Grandma. I wanted to give the other kids a chance to play,"
Omar gently told me after.
"Grandma, I don't think Omar was fair to me," I said.
"Caleb, I'm sorry to hear that. I'm sure there's a good reason why. Remember, God wants us to forgive each other," explained Grandma.

(Circle) the correct answer, for questions 1-4 below.

1. Caleb and Omar are _____.
a. happy
b. best friends
c. playing ball

2. How was Caleb feeling?
a. Joyful
b. Excited
c. Upset

3. Should Caleb *forgive* Omar? Write to explain why.
a. Yes
b. No
Explain: _____

4. How should Caleb show that he forgives Omar?
a. Be kind and talk to him.
b. Look away and don't talk to him.
c. Don't play freeze tag together.

5. What does it mean to <u>forgive?</u>

_____
_____

Sprinkle Joy
Publishing
www.sprinklejoybooks.com

Grandma smiled. "Hanna, say what's in your heart. God is always here to listen. When you pray, say what you're thankful for and remember how you care for others. There's power in praying!"

# READING COMPREHENSION

**"I thank You, Lord, with all my heart."**
(Psalm 138:1 GNT)

Directions: After Reading the story, answer the questions.

I sat in Grandma's favorite chair. It smelled like her vanilla scent and made me think of her kind words and soft voice.

I started to cry again. *I wished I could've stayed at the hospital with Grandma. I wished there was something I could do to help make her better. That's it! I know what I can do! I can pray for Grandma to get better! That's right. There's power in praying.* I joined Caleb, and we prayed for Grandma.

1. What happened to Grandma?
a. She went shopping.
b. She stayed in the hospital.
c. She visited friends in the hospital.

2. Why was Hanna crying?

_____

_____

3. How is Hanna going to make things better?
a. By praying.
b. By continuing to cry.
c. By sleeping.

4. Write a prayer that Hanna could pray to God for Grandma.
**Dear God,**

_____

_____

_____

_____

Sprinkle Joy
Publishing
www.sprinklejoybooks.com

**Directions: Color the characters as they pray to God and write the name of someone you can pray for today.**

Today, I am praying for _____.

"Let us keep our eyes fixed on Jesus, on Whom our Faith depends, beginning to end." (Hebrews 12:2 GNT)

GRATEFUL thankful BLESSED

HOLY BIBLE

GOD IS LOVE!

 # Bible Verses:

*"God is love, and those who live in love live in union with God and God lives in union with them."*
(1 John 4:16 GNT)

*"We love because God first loved us."*
(1 John 4:19 GNT)

*"God showed His love for us by sending His only Son into the world, so that we might have life through Him."*
(1 John 4:9 GNT)

*"The Lord and the Lord alone is our God. Love the Lord your God with all your heart, with all your soul, and with all your strength."*
(Deuteronomy 6:4-5 GNT)

*"The Lord is merciful and loving, slow to become angry and full of constant love."*
(Psalms 103:8 GNT)

*"But for those who honor the Lord, his love lasts forever."*
(Psalms 103:17 GNT)

*"Let us love one another, because love comes from God. Whoever loves is a child of God and knows God. Whoever does not love does not know God, for God is love."*
(1 John 4:7-8 GNT)

# GOD IS LOVE WORD MATCH-UP

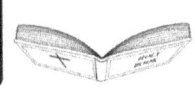

**Directions:** Read and complete the word definition match up. Draw a line to match.

| Words | Definitions |
|-------|-------------|
| Believe | To be thankful and appreciate good things in life. |
| Grateful | To forgive and not punish someone. |
| Mercy | Free gift, and favor from God working in you. |
| Peace | Almighty creator of the world and everything in it. |
| Values | To believe and trust in the hope and blessings of God. |
| Virtues | People who believe in Jesus Christ our Savior, the Son of God. |
| Christians | To speak sharing your thoughts and listen to God. |
| Faith | To trust and have confidence in God. |
| God | Putting others before yourself, seeing good qualities in people and valuing them. |
| Grace | A feeling of happiness, a fruit of the Spirit. |
| Hope | To live in harmony with no violence or war. |
| Joy | Qualities that motivate our character and behavior that help us make decisions. |
| Love | Good characteristics we demonstrate, actions or behaviors to benefit someone else. |
| Pray | To trust, have faith that something exists that is true and good. |

# GOD IS LOVE - WORDS TO KNOW # 1

| Christians | People who believe in Jesus Christ our Savior, the Son of God. |
| Faith | To believe and trust in the hope and blessings of God. |
| God | Almighty creator of the world and everything in it. |
| Grace | Free gift, and favor from God working in you. |
| Hope | To trust and have confidence in God. |
| Joy | A feeling of happiness, a fruit of the Spirit. |
| Love | Putting others before yourself, seeing good qualities in people and valuing them. |
| Pray | To speak sharing your thoughts and listen to God. |

Sprinkle Joy
Publishing
www.sprinklejoybooks.com

# GOD IS LOVE - WORDS TO KNOW # 2

| Believe | To trust, have faith that something exists that is true and good. |
| Grateful | To be thankful and appreciate good things in life. |
| Mercy | To forgive and not punish someone. |
| Patience | To be kind and gentle and not give up hope. |
| Peace | To live in harmony with no violence or war. |
| Prayer | To talk to God and listen to God. |
| Values | Qualities that motivate our character and behavior that help us make decisions. |
| Virtues | Good characteristics we demonstrate, actions or behaviors to benefit someone else. |

"Love the Lord our God with all your heart,
with all your soul, with all your mind,
and with all your strength.
Love your neighbor as you love yourself.
There is no other commandment more important
than these two."
*(Matthew 22:34-40 GNT)*
*(Mark 12:30-34 GNT)*
*(Luke 10:25-28 GNT)*

"PEACE BE WITH YOU."

John 20:19 GNT

**Thank you for your purchase!**
**Please leave an honest review. We read every review**
**and they help new readers discover our books.**

*Order Sprinkle Joy Publishing Books*
www.sprinklejoybooks.com

**"Out of the fullness of His grace He has blessed us all,**
**giving us one blessing after another."**
**(John 1:16 GNT)**